Prin

A play

Andrew Davies

Samuel French – London
New York – Sydney – Toronto – Hollywood

PRIN

First presented at the Lyric, Hammersmith, on 23rd
August, 1989 with the following cast:

Prin	Sheila Hancock
Dibs	Susie Blake
Boyle	Paul Copley
Walker	John Michie
Kite	David Howey
Melanie	Victoria Worsley

Directed by **Richard Wilson**
Designed by **Julian McGowan**
Lighting by **Kevin Sleep**
Movement by **Geraldine Stephenson**

The play subsequently transferred to the Lyric, Shaftes-
bury Avenue, London, presented by Robert Cogo-
Fawcett for Lyric Hammersmith Productions and
Showstarters with the following cast:

Prin	Sheila Hancock
Dibs	Susie Blake
Boyle	Paul Copley
Walker	John Michie
Kite	David Howey
Melanie	Susie Lindeman

Directed by **Richard Wilson**
Designed by **Julian McGowan**

CHARACTERS

Prin, aged 58
Dibs, aged 39
Walker, aged 32
Kite, aged 48
Boyle, aged 43
Melanie, aged 20

The action of the play takes place in Prin's room

ACT I   Monday morning

ACT II   Monday afternoon

Time—the present

ACT I

Prin's room at college. Monday morning

There is a large desk and a window

Prin sits, not at the desk. She is smoking and reading the previous day's "Observer". Dibs stands looking out of the window

Prin (*after a few moments*) God Almighty. (*After a moment; reading from the paper*) "It may be easy enough for a mother just to keep on dishing out food and clean T-shirts and hoping that they'll come in by morning. But a father, mediating as he does between the world and the family, has to have an Attitude to What's Going On."

Pause

Are you there? Anyone at home?

Dibs You know I'm here, Prin.

Prin That's a relief. I thought your soul might have left your body. Just popped out for a little flight around the playing fields.

Dibs (*turning*) Oh, that's nice. I wish it could. "Hallo, Mr Blackbird, how are you today?" "And who in tarnation might you be?" (*The blackbird sounds like Uncle Remus: Dibs is good at imitations*) "Oh, I'm Dibbie's soul, just out for a little trip to see the world!" "Well you just better get right on back into her pretty little head, there's company at home and someone wants to talk to you."

Prin turns her head slowly and gives her a long withering stare

Sorry.

Prin Fifteen years of Early Language Acquisition have rotted your brain.

Dibs Yes, I s'pose they have, rather. Sorry.

Prin (*conceding*) That blackbird wasn't bad.

Dibs (*pleased*) Did you like him? He's a new one.

Prin Ration his appearances. Once a month should be sufficient.

Dibs All right.

Prin Dr Bile, on the other hand, we find we need at least once a week.

Dibs All right.

Prin Well then?

Dibs Not now, Prin.

Prin "I am not in the vein." eh? You little prima donna.

Dibs Not a job lot, anyway.

Prin turns and looks at her again

Prin No; definitely not a job lot.

What she is expressing is love. They hold the look, then Dibs turns to the window again

What did you think of it? Did you read it?

Dibs What?

Prin This. Father mediating as he does between the world and the family.

Dibs Yes. I did read it actually.

Prin What did you think of it?

Dibs Bit iffy.

Prin You thought it was a bit iffy.

Dibs Well in point of fact it was pretty naff, really.

Prin You've been talking to the students again. I will not have you talking to the students, you keep picking up these nasty little infections of the vocabulary.

Dibs Sorry. Actually I thought it was disgraceful.

Prin And you were right. D'you know I *taught* that girl *for two years in the sixth form*?

Dibs Yes, we do all know that, Prin.

Prin God knows why I admit to it, it doesn't reflect well on me at all. She was silly then and she's sillier now. Her concept of gender roles is fixated at the level of Ladybird books circa nineteen fifty. Jane helps Mummy in the kitchen. Peter helps Daddy with the car. Father mediates between the world and the family. She deserves five years hard labour.

Dibs Mm. Right. Two years before the mast, with fifty lashes a day and keelhauling on Sundays.

Prin I am being absolutely serious. The Secretary of State for Education sees no case at present for raising the salaries of teachers. "I am well aware that there are shortcomings in teacher supply", he said, "but distressingly large numbers of people still seem prepared to use the State system rather than go private, and we wouldn't want to be seen to be encouraging them."

Dibs He didn't say that, did he?

Prin More or less, more or less. It's like Ethiopia you see. Enough people seem to want to be Ethiopians as it is, so we shouldn't send them any aid, it only encourages them.

Dibs He didn't say *that*.

Prin He implied it. What's so fascinating out there?

Dibs Nothing.

Prin A likely tale.

Dibs They're coming back from early training.

Prin Ah. Back from the morning gallops. Their long manes tossing gently in the breeze, a light sweat shimmering on their glossy flanks, no doubt?

Dibs Bit far to see, Prin.

Prin In these matters one sees what one wishes to see. One sees what one feels to be there. The light sweat will be shimmering on the glossy flanks, don't you worry. Some things, thank God, don't change.

The intercom on her desk bleeps

Describe them to me.

Dibs Aren't you going to pick up?

Prin Describe them to me.

Dibs Well . . .

It bleeps again. Prin answers

Prin Principal. (*Pause*) No, of course I can't. I'm in conference till ten, then I'm addressing the finalists. I have a very full day. (*Pause*) All right, I'll give him five minutes at ten forty-five, if it's so frightfully urgent. (*She puts down the receiver*) Bile.

Dibs Oh.

Prin Wonder what *he* wants now.

Dibs Well. Er, in point of fact . . .

Prin In point of what?

Dibs Um, Prin . . .

Prin Oh, never mind him, let's think about pleasant things while we have the chance. Who's been out for the dawn gallop? How are they looking, Dibs?

Dibs Well. Little Betty Brain, bouncing up and down like a yoyo . . . Maggie Savage . . . black sweatband round her forehead and her T-shirt says "No".

Prin Good.

Dibs That wispy one with the old-fashioned face I can never remember the name of . . . long jumper.

Prin Garment or event?

Dibs Both.

Prin Melinda Peebles.

Dibs Oh, yes.

Prin Who else?

Dibs Why don't you come and look for yourself?

Prin I don't need to. Go on.

Dibs Oninka Small.

Prin Good.

Dibs And Julie Cinnamon and that's the lot.

Prin Ah. Julie Cinnamon. Your favourite.

Dibs I don't have favourites, Prin.

Prin You *don't have favourites*? Are you telling me that you have totally lost all your powers of fine discrimination?

Dibs No, I'm not telling you that, Prin.

Prin I am glad to hear it. Where would you be now if I didn't have favourites?

Dibs No idea.

Prin Don't be *airy* about it, little Dibs. I have a very good idea. I picture you on a coach, Dibs, a coach in a traffic jam in a slum, on its way to some dreadful gritty wasteland municipal playing fields on the edge of the dead city, overlooked by ravaged tower blocks and gasometers. The coach would be full of small-eyed foul-mouthed tattooed inner-city schoolgirls. Some would be fighting, some singing, some making provocative, meant-to-be-heard comments about your clothes, your habits, and your imagined private life, which would indeed need to be imagined. Not one of these girls would have a crush on you. These unhealthy fixations are happily much rarer in co-educational schools, and in any case, all the free-floating fantasies would be scooped, so to speak, by the fair curly-haired colleague, twenty years your junior, who sits merrily prattling by your side.

Dibs She sounds interesting.

Prin Not a chance. She's happily married to a junior manager in the Halifax Building Society, and is also conducting a *liaison dangereuse* with the ... yes, with the *woodwork* master, the one with the shavings clinging like paper curlers to the hair on his muscular forearms.

Dibs Oh.

Prin That's where you'd be if we didn't have favourites. Dibs, you'd be an ordinary teacher in an ordinary state school. Not a deputy principal at one of the last and best of the independent Colleges of Education.

Dibs We are not independent Prin.

Prin We allow the LEA to foot the *bill*, Dibs, but apart from that we do what we damn well like. Well naturally. And all this *is* yours, Dibs, with a very nice cottage in the Cotswolds for weekends as well.

Dibs Not to mention the privilege of daily bullying and abuse from one of the finest intellects of her generation.

Prin Oh I say. Well, quite. Not to mention that.

Dibs It's all right. I know why you're being so foul to me.

Prin Do you?

Dibs Yes I do.

Pause

Prin Well, if you're refusing to stake a claim, I'll certainly nominate Julie Cinnamon as my favourite for this year. There are several interesting things about Julie Cinnamon. I've been looking at her file. I was pleased to see that one's impression of balance and symmetry are borne out by the figures. D'you know her measured IQ is precisely equal to her weight in pounds?

Dibs Is it now?

Prin Mm. A hundred and forty-one. Her height is five foot ten and a quarter. I do love that little extra quarter inch, don't you?

Dibs Quite indifferent to it, in point of fact.

Prin I don't believe a word of it. You're a fiend for detail.

Dibs What's her reach then?

Prin Her what?

Dibs Her reach. (*She extends both arms sideways*) Wingtip to wingtip.

Pause

Prin Quite long enough, I should imagine.

Dibs I know why you're doing this.

Prin Do you. "Her pure and eloquent blood Spoke in her cheeks, and so distinctly wrought, That one might almost say, her body thought."

Dibs You said that to me once.

Prin I said it to you just now.
Dibs I mean, you said it about me.
Prin And now I'm trying it out on Julie Cinnamon.

Pause

Dibs I've been ... I've been hoping we could have a talk.
Prin We are having a talk.
Dibs I mean a real talk.
Prin Oh, one of those, a real old-fashioned let your hair down heart-to-heart, eh?
Dibs If you like.
Prin Mind-to-mind a bit too taxing for us, is it? You tried to start a conversation at the breakfast table, didn't you?
Dibs Yes, I did, I'm sorry.
Prin Silence and *The Guardian* until the second cigarette.
Dibs They didn't deliver *The Guardian*.
Prin We had yesterday's *Observer*. Transgress one boundary, you'll transgress them all. Bear it in mind.
Dibs Actually ... in point of fact ... that's what I wanted to talk about. Crossing boundaries.
Prin You crossed one this morning all right. What the hell *was* that we had for breakfast?
Dibs Oh, that. Er, "Fruit 'n' Fibre".
Prin *What?*
Dibs "Fruit 'n' Fibre". (*As if to excuse it*) Kelloggs make it.
Prin "Fruit ... 'n' ... Fibre". I see. (*She pauses*) Some sort of symbolic gesture, was it, little Dibs? A homely metaphor for our relationship? Plump little sultana peeping shyly from the *roughage*?
Dibs Not at all.
Prin It tasted like the sweepings of the factory floor.
Dibs (*sharply*) What would you know about the sweepings of the factory floor?
Prin What would either of us know?
Dibs Look, I'm sorry. It was just an idea, the "Fruit 'n' Fibre". There's no need to make so much of it. All right?
Prin Nothing is without significance.
Dibs Well if you want to know I just couldn't face grilling the kippers this morning.
Prin (*softening*) Little Dibs. Little Dibs. If you can't face up to a pair of kippers, what can you face up to in this cruel world.
Dibs (*playing the game*) I know, I know, it's so shaming. But it was their glum faces, Prin. So resigned to their fate, you know? And one of them turned his sad ole eye to me, and said: (*Scottish accent, good, as before*) "Dae it to us quick, Miss Dibs, we ken fu' well ye widnae wanta see us suffer. We understand it is nae personal." (*After a pause*) God. I am a grown woman. Why can't I say what I want to say? I sometimes wish you wouldn't call me Little Dibs, Prin.
Prin But you are Little Dibs. What else would I call you?

Dibs My name's Dorothy.

Prin So it is. I never felt it suited you. Whoever heard of a linnet called Dorothy?

Dibs I'm not a linnet, I'm a woman, Prin.

Prin So prosaic all of a sudden. Dorothy. You want to be called Dorothy now, do you?

Dibs You called me that once.

Prin That was before I knew you; that was before I . . . gave you substance. Didn't there use to be something called a Dorothy bag? I was never quite sure what it was. I imagine something soft and velvety, don't you? No shape to it. A sort of amorphous *pouch* thing, with a drawstring, that you could hang from your belt. Full of useful little things like darning kits and Elastoplast and aspirins, and little keepsakes. Sentimental value only. Nothing with exchange potential on the open market. And now you want to be called Dorothy again.

Dibs It's really not all that important.

Prin Don't back off. We're having a talk.

Dibs You're having a talk. I'm embroidering round the edges.

Prin Well, that's the kind of talk we have.

Dibs These days.

Prin I went a bit far a few minutes ago. I got a bit carried away on that school bus. I still like that cardigan.

Dibs Thank you.

Prin Positano.

Dibs Yes.

Prin Yes.

Dibs You sat me down in the café and told me you'd forgotten something, and you trailed all the way back to that desperately expensive shop for it, and I hadn't even seen you see me longing for it.

Prin I've always kept a sharp eye out for anything you might be longing for. The hatchet-faced girl in the hotel Sorrento, for example.

Dibs Rubbish, I wasn't interested at all.

Prin She was interested in you.

Dibs Rubbish. (*She pauses*) Prin, can we have a proper talk?

Prin God. A proper talk. How dull that sounds. Can't we have an improper talk? We haven't had an improper talk for days.

Dibs Prin.

Prin Little pig, little pig, will you let me come in?

Pause

Dibs I haven't picked the right day have I?

Prin Monday. I've never feared Mondays. I have always—how did your mother put it? I've always had my washing out by half-past nine.

Dibs What is it? Is it that meeting?

Prin That meeting? It's just another meeting. Meetings are nothing. They confirm understandings arrived at previously. I shan't even attend that meeting. I shall confirm the position with Kite before lunch, and leave him to manipulate the meeting.

Dibs Don't you think we should at least give him lunch?

Prin I don't want to have lunch with Kite. I want to have lunch with you.

Dibs Oh dear.

Prin Is the prospect so gloomy, little Dibs?

Dibs No, it's just I assumed you'd ... and there's a sort of Departmental lunch ...

Prin Biological Sciences are having a lunch?

Dibs Just a little one.

Prin Dr Bile is dipping into the Hospitality fund?

Dibs Well, not really ...

Prin I see, just bringing along a few frogs and rabbits from the lab.

Dibs I could get out of it, I s'pose.

Prin No, no. I wouldn't deprive you of the company of Dr Bile. I shall just have to muddle through on my own. Or perhaps I could command the company of one or two key students. Julie Cinnamon, for example.

Dibs Yes, that'd be nice.

Prin I'm only teasing you, little Dibs.

Dibs I really wouldn't mind. Honestly.

Prin That's a strange word.

Dibs What?

Prin "Honestly."

Dibs So's "teasing".

Prin You think I'm worried, don't you? I am not worried. Everything is under control. It's going to be rather a tiresome day that's all. Finalists, Bile, Kite, even a heart-to-heart with little Dibs if we get round to it, but hardly a worrying day.

Dibs Change. Change is worrying, isn't it?

Prin But nothing's going to change. Not here. Nothing has changed since I began. I am going to keep things like this. D'you know who wrote that?

Dibs No.

Prin The Poet Laureate.

Dibs Not very poetic.

Prin Such a stubborn little soul. (*She looks at her watch*) And now you've wasted all the time I was going to spend preparing my address to the Finalists.

Dibs You'll think of something.

Prin No doubt I will.

Prin goes and gets her academic gown and puts it on. Dibs watches her as she composes herself: she puts on extra authority with the gown. Dibs still, after all this time, regards her with a little awe. Then Prin turns. 10 a.m.

Little pig, little pig, will you let me come in?

Dibs No, no, by the hairs on my chinny-chin-chin.

Prin Good.

Dibs Prin.

Prin What?

Dibs I *have* got hairs on my chinny-chin-chin.

Prin Of course you have. So have I. But they are immaterial. (*She steps* *forward to address the finalists. She is in fact addressing the audience)*

Dibs exits

Four years ago, you came to this college for the first time to be trained for the profession of teaching. Most of you were fresh from school, full of fine A level grades and vague ideals about helping society; some of you were just lifting up your heads from the milky confusion of bearing and rearing your own children. You may remember that time, that first time that we met. I remember that time. I told you then that from the point of view of common sense, you were embarking on something ridiculous. Why should anyone of any intelligence prepare herself for a career in education, in a society that has lost all faith in itself; a society in which a streak of cynical contempt for all civilized values runs straight through from what our leaders please to call the top to the bottom; in a nation whose people express their feelings about the future through a falling birthrate and a passion for newspaper bingo? I seem to recall I laid it on a bit strong more or less along those lines. And I don't see that anything's happened in the last four years to make me change my mind. What with the falling birthrate and the successive cuts imposed by one government after another, you would have done much better to go off and get yourselves pregnant, so that there would be some children around for you to educate when you finally qualified. Some of you didn't quite grasp that I was making a rhetorical point. However: the rest of you are here. And you have spent four years in the pursuit of excellence. And you are, all of you, excellent. Though some are more excellent than others. And most of you have jobs to go to, teaching jobs in the state system. You are fortunate—most people would disagree. You're going to be teachers in the most ignorant, the most philistine country in Europe. East or West. Our rulers treat the educational system they administer with derision, starving it of resources while they buy for their own children the privilege they themselves enjoyed. You will be underpaid and undervalued. You will be harassed by little jacks-in-office. You will be slandered and vilified by the most ignorant and prejudiced Press in the world. It's beginning to sound quite a bit of fun, isn't it? And it will be. It will be. Deep down, they're all frightened of you, because you know what you're about, and they don't. You're stepping out into the world full of the power that being changed can give. And you are going to change others whatever they do to you. However they try to shackle you. Remember. A teacher possesses extraordinary power. They know it. They fear it. You can do it. They can't. Eventually they have to go away. They have to go away and leave you with the children. And then it begins. What are you going to do with it? What are you going to do with the future? Be extraordinary. Let your lessons be forms of life worth living for their own sake. Be extraordinary. Show them how to be extraordinary people. I am an extraordinary person. You are extraordinary people, because I say you are. There are not many of us. Not yet. Propagate your kind. Good luck. (*She stares at her audience for a few moments. Then goes back, as it were. To her room. She takes off her gown, chucks it over something, then collapses into a chair,*

*sitting inelegantly, her knees apart, the way some older academic women do.
She lights a cigarette)* Stiffener. *(She looks over to the cupboard. Thinks
about getting up and going over to it. Changes her mind. Calling)* Dibs. Are
you still lurking about?

Dibs comes in

Dibs Hallo, I've just got back.
Prin Stiffener, please Dibs.

*Dibs goes to the cupboard. Whisky bottle, soda syphon, glass. She makes Prin
a stiff one as they talk*

Back from where? You haven't been *teaching* again, have you?
Dibs No, I took Monty for a walk. Lovely out.
Prin Did he bite anyone?
Dibs No he didn't, he's really not bad at all these days, in point of fact. He
did rather menace the hammer throwers for a bit, but it was just his fun.
We, er, met John Boyle.
Prin *(taking her drink)* Dr Bile taking the air? That's a grim thought. And
Monty didn't bite him?
Dibs No, he didn't.
Prin Growled at him though, I'll bet.
Dibs Didn't actually.
Prin Gave him the stiff-legged stare?
Dibs Not really, no.
Prin That dog is beginning to give me cause for concern. I suppose Bile was
out looking for specimens. All the wee sleekit cowering timorous beasties
trembling under the hedgerows at the approach of Dr Bile's squelchy
crêpe-soled creepers. Did he have his little blowpipe with the poison
darts?
Dibs Not as far as I could see. How did it go? The talk to the finalists.
Prin They stared at me mildly. Dibs, like goldfish. Don't change the subject.
What was Bile up to? Did he speak to you?
Dibs Well, he did actually.
Prin What about?
Dibs Oh, you know. This and that. He, um, he walked along with us, in
point of fact.
Prin In point of *what*?
Dibs Fact . . . sorry.

Pause

Prin You are telling me that you have been for a walk with Dr Bile.
Dibs Well, s'pose I am. In a way. (*Just a shade of defiance*)
Prin Little Dibs, when I slipped you into the Science Education department, I did it out of compassion, to find you somewhere warm and dry,
even a linnet can't spend her whole life on the playing fields. And, of
course, to spy on Bile. But you're taking it far beyond the call of duty.
You don't have to socialize with the little shit.

Dibs He's not all that bad. When you get to know him. Actually I think he's softened quite a bit.

Prin Yes, perhaps he has. The image of a sweaty middle-aged Camembert comes to mind.

Dibs Oh, Prin. Don't.

Prin It's you that's softening. You need a refresher course. Do Bile for me.

Dibs Oh, no, not now. I don't feel like it.

Prin I've got to see him in person in a minute. I want a booster shot. Come on, little Dibs. It isn't very often that I ask you for something, is it? Please.

Dibs Oh, all right, which one d'you want?

Prin The rat.

Dibs Oh, no, not that one, Prin.

Prin The rat, the female rat! (*She prompts*) "Ladies and gentlemen . . ."

There is some hesitation before Dibs starts, she doesn't really want to

Dibs (*in a Northern accent*) Ladies and gentlemen, you have observed my dissection of the female rat. Now I shall come amongst you and observe *your* dissection of the . . . (*Little frisson*) female rat.

Prin Good. Don't forget the sniff.

Dibs essays a phlegmy sniff

Dibs Please do not be squeamish. The rat feels nothing. The rat is not a rat any more. It is a piece of decaying tissue. (*A little gulp. She feels a bit sick*) It might even happen during the course of my observation, that part of my body will make accidental contact with part of your body. When this happens, I will recoil immediately, and scuttle straight back to my desk. If you find this puzzling, let me explain that is how I do it. That is how I make love. I learnt it from the rats, you know. Rats are very quick. (*In her own voice*) Ba-boom!

Prin Very good. On.

Dibs No.

Prin "I may seem . . ."

Dibs I expect I may seem a bit of a cold fish to you, but there is one thing that gets me going. (*Pause. She is feeling nauseous. It takes an effort to get it out. When she says it, it's half her own voice, half the Bile imitation*) The splayed genitalia of the female rat. Excuse me.

She puts her hand to her mouth and runs out

Prin Well, well, well. (*She goes to the phone, picks up the receiver*) I'll see Dr Boyle now. If he's here. (*She puts the phone down. Thoughtfully*) The splayed genitalia of the female rat.

Boyle comes in. 10.45

Dr Bile.

Boyle Boyle.

Prin Of course.

Boyle sniffs his fruity sniff

She never gets it *quite* right.

Boyle Sorry, Principal?

Prin Nothing.

Boyle It's very good of you to give me a moment, Principal. Busy day. Thought we should have a little word about CATE, though (*Dibs's imitation of him was very good*)

Prin About Kate.

Boyle That's right.

Prin Which Kate would that be? Kate Hargreaves, Kate Spencer-Curtis? Katie Oluwenga? Plain Kate, bonny Kate, Kate the curst, Kate of Kate Hall, we have so many Kates here, you can hardly expect me to guess which one's your favourite, Dr Boyle.

Boyle I don't have favourites, Principal.

Prin Oh?

Boyle In point of fact.

Prin In point of what?

Boyle Fact.

Prin I see.

Boyle does another fruity sniff

Boyle CATE's an acronym, Principal, as we both know very well. Council for the Accreditation of Teacher Education.

Prin Oh, *them.*

Boyle I think we'd do well to take them very seriously.

Prin Those two dim little men who were here last month? Mr Soames and Mr Sodd, was it? You take them as seriously as you like, Dr Boyle.

Boyle I think we should, Principal. They can close down courses. Faculties. Whole colleges. I've, er, heard a little buzz.

Prin How very nice for you.

Boyle I thought you ought to know. We're going to get a mixed report. Science Education gets the thumbs up. Relevance, accountability, classroom cred. (*Another sniff*) One or two of the other departments don't er, meet the criteria.

Prin I am glad to hear it. Our criteria are to do with the pursuit of excellence, with Forms of Life worth living for their own sake. Those two little men wouldn't know a Form of Life if it *bit them in the leg.*

Boyle But the local authorities and the DEs take them ...

Prin Very very seriously?

Boyle Well yes. They do. In point of fact.

Prin In *what* of fact.

Boyle I'm just trying to help, Principal.

Prin *Are* you.

Boyle Yes.

Prin Then I'm very grateful, Dr Boyle.

Boyle They've, er, co-opted me on to the committee for the merger meeting this afternoon.

Prin Oh, dear. What a bore for you. I am sorry.

Boyle As a non-voting member, of course.

Prin Responsibility without power, eh? So much nicer the other way round, I always think.

Boyle I was wondering if there was any particular line you'd like me to take. About the merger.

Prin There isn't going to be a merger. And of course, you must speak as the heart dictates. If you feel that you could manage that, Dr Bile.

Boyle Boyle, Principal. My name is Boyle.

Prin Of *course* it is. I'm sorry, Dr Boyle, I'm not getting any younger, I can't be expected to remember every little thing.

Boyle I've been here ten years.

Prin Yes, I'm sure you have, but we have got rather a busy morning, there's nothing I'd like better than a good old chat about old times.

Boyle What I meant was: after ten years, don't you think the joke's wearing a little thin?

Prin Joke?

Boyle Pretending not to remember my name.

Prin Ah. You don't find it amusing.

Boyle Not really Principal. It doesn't really bother me either if that's what you're thinking.

Prin Well, that seems most satisfactory, I can be amused without your being bothered, now I have got to address Academic Board in five minutes, so if there was anything pressing?

Pause

Boyle Has Dorothy Minns had a word with you at all?

Prin The Vice-Principal and I discuss many things, Dr Bile, from the nature of perceived reality to kippers and rats, we have many words together, and we would like to think of most of them as private, was there anything particular you had in mind, Dr Bile?

Boyle Boyle, Principal.

Pause

It doesn't matter.

He turns and goes

A dog growls off, growls and then barks

Prin Thank you Monty; *much* better. (*She goes upstage and puts her gown on again*)

A long table covered with a dark cloth, bowl of flowers on it, appears downstage. Two chairs

Prin comes slowly downstage and sits at the table facing the audience

Dibs scuttles on and takes the chair by her side. Dibs has a file full of papers. She whispers to Prin

Prin listens. She gives the audience a long considering look. She shakes her head to Dibs, then clears her throat

I've called this extraordinary meeting of Academic Board to make two statements. One short one, and one rather longer one. First the merger question. The College is not prepared to consider a merger: we are not here to have our assets stripped. Thirty years of the pursuit of excellence are not going to vanish into the belly of the Polytechnic, nor are they going to be sucked into the maw of a mediocre university. Some of our sister institutions have dithered, and been destroyed, some have allowed themselves to be seduced by promises of parity. Where are they now? Our policy, as always, is to be bloody, bold and resolute. So much for that.

Dibs whispers, drawing her attention to a hand up

No Dr Boyle, I'm not prepared to accept discussion on that one. Tell it to the Merger Committee this afternoon. Now I want to go on to something *much* more interesting. Rumours have been circulating the college about a number of photographs of a certain nature discovered in a student's room. Since prurient speculation and fevered fantasy are all too palpably affecting the quality of your work, I propose to put you in the picture. So to speak. Was that a giggle, Mr Hoole? If I were you I'd wait till I'd got tenure before I risked a giggle. The facts are these. In pursuing their investigations into the possession of soft drugs, the police were allowed to search certain rooms in Radclyffe Hall. They did not find any drugs. In one student's bedroom, however, they found a collection of photographs, which brought to my attention. The subject of the photographs was one of the students of the college. Some of them featured a second person as well. The, er, the technical quality of the photography was very good indeed. Culturally, it seemed to me and to Sergeant Cadwallader that they could be divided into three categories. Some of them could only be described as ... very good photographs. (*A pause after this enigmatic remark*) A second group manifested a strong preoccupation with the erotic; they reminded me rather of the work of Fuseli, and they reminded Sergeant Cadwallader of someone called Bob Guccione, an artist unknown to me. The third group I would describe as cheerfully priapic. Sergeant Cadwallader thought that they might warrant a prosecution under the Obscene Publications Act. I pointed out to the Sergeant that the only act of publication was his, when he showed them to me, but that I preferred not to proceed against him. Nevertheless, I told him, this sort of thing is an intolerable intrusion into the private leisure activities of members of this college. Sergeant Cadwallader got a fit of the sulks and took himself off. I think that's all. Except that perhaps we should congratulate Mrs Heritage on the success of her 2nd year option course in Creative Photography. (*She looks up*) Ah no, Dr Crossman, I don't think we need any discussion on this issue either. Well, ladies and gentlemen, I shan't keep you any longer. We all of us have excellence to pursue. Meeting concluded. (*She gets up and moves upstage*)

Dibs stays for a moment or two. She gives a little apologetic shrug to the audience, then moves upstage back to Prin's office. Prin takes off her gown and chucks it, as before. Dibs stands hesitantly as Prin goes to sit at the desk

The table and chairs disappear

Still trailing along, little Dibs? Nothing to do? Have all the reports been

written? All the waste paper collected, all the flowers sent to all the
sickbeds, all the little charity envelopes sealed? You could always cut your
toe-nails, you know.

Dibs I was wondering if we might have that talk now, Prin.

Prin Ah. Unfortunately not. I've been bagged by little Dick Walker.

Dibs Oh. Right, fine, sorry.

Prin You can bag me later. You and I have a whole life yawning ahead of us
to talk in.

Dibs Right, then.

Dibs goes

Prin (*softly*) Little pig, little pig ... (*She picks up the phone*) I'll see Mr
Walker now. (*She replaces the receiver*)

Growling and snarling off

*Walker, a pleasant-looking man in his thirties, comes in fast, panicky, off-
balance*

(*Affably*) That's right, Mr Walker. Do come in. Make yourself at home.
Sit on a chair. Lie on the floor if you wish.

Walker Er ... thanks. (*He sits down. He looks around nervously*) Haven't
been in here since my interview.

Prin Well, that wasn't so long ago, was it? About a week?

Walker Three years, actually.

Prin As long as that. Well, here you are again.

Walker Yes.

A slight pause

Prin Was that all then, Mr Walker?

Walker No! No. Er, no. (*He looks at her, laughs nervously, goes through
some brief physical routine, clasps his hands together, seems about to speak,
doesn't*)

Prin Take your time, Mr Walker. I'll just browse through a volume or two
of Proust while I'm waiting.

Walker Sorry. Well, um. It's a bit embarrassing. Personal. You know.

Prin Do I, Mr Walker?

Walker Confidential.

Prin Ah. You have a confession to make.

Walker How did you guess?

Prin Experience, Mr Walker. Light years of experience. And my advice is,
think before you speak. It may not be possible for me to respect your
confidentiality. I may find it expedient to shout it from the rooftops. Not
very likely, of course. I've never shouted from a rooftop in my life.
Something I'm saving for my old age, if ever, like golf and the novels of
Walter Scott, had time to think?

Walker Yes. I don't see how ... telling you could make things any worse. In
fact ... your statement at Academic Board rather cheered me up.

Prin So *you've* been posing for filthy postcards too.

Walker No! No, Principal.

Prin So what have you been up to, then?

Walker Well, it's rather difficult I've been well you see in a way I suppose you could say in a sense I've been having an affair with a student. (*All that came out in a breath*)

Prin In what sense.

Walker Well. The usual sense.

Prin I'd like us to be clear about this, Mr Walker. You're telling me that you've been having sexual intercourse with one of the students.

Walker Yes, I am, Principal. (*After a pause*) Sorry.

Pause

Prin Mr Walker. I'm very disappointed in you.

Walker Er . . . sorry.

Prin You seemed such an interesting young man at your interview. I had hoped you were going to develop into a prima donna. Now I find you're just another job lot. What a very average thing to do. I assume you've got a wife at home, I seem to remember one of those?

Walker Yes I have, Principal. I'm really terribly——

Prin Oh do shut up, Mr Walker. So you have this wife, pleasant intelligent young woman, you met her at University no doubt, two young children, no doubt, am I right?

Walker Yes.

Prin There you are, you see! All you English chaps are exactly the same! You all have wives and two young children languishing on some estate, reading Jane Austen and Alison Lurie amongst the nappy buckets and soggy rusks.

Walker George Eliot. Actually. Mostly. Sorry.

She gives him a look and sweeps on

Prin You all have vague ideas for major books you'll never write.

Walker Well . . . maybe not a major book, but——

Prin Spare me the book, Mr Walker, it will never be written. Because it's so much easier, so much less bother, to turn your classroom into a swamp of sensuality. They're a bit exhausting, aren't they, the long haul of marriage, and the steady slog of scholarship.

Walker Yes, they are.

Prin So you let them go, eh, and console yourself by slaking your lust on the bodies of the fine young women so thoughtfully provided for your use.

Walker No, it wasn't like that, honestly.

Prin What was it like, then, Mr Walker. Surprise me. Who's the girl? Julie Cinnamon?

Walker (*surprised*) No.

Prin Don't you teach Julie Cinnamon?

Walker Er, yes, yes I do, actually.

Prin What's the matter then? Don't you like her?

Walker Yes, very much. Er, brilliant student.

Prin But you fear the pinnacles of life.

Walker Sorry?

Prin You went for one of the job lots.

Walker No!

Prin Who did you go for then?

Walker No, I meant no, it's not right. Talking about, talking about prima donnas and job lots. I mean everyone's valuable. Everyone's ... worth something. Everyone's unique.

Prin Oh, yes. But some are more unique than others, and to hell with Fowler's *Modern English Usage*. All right, Mr Walker, tell me about the unique and valuable person.

Walker Well ...

Prin Just a moment. (*She picks up the phone, presses a button*) Miss Minns, could you step in here a moment.

Walker Oh no, I couldn't, not with her here.

Prin The Vice-Principal doesn't get much fun, Mr Walker. She is a reliable witness, in case either of us wants to go to law about this. And she does love a good story. I know she's in Science Education now, but her first love was ever the oral transmission of folklore I believe. She did her MA Dissertation on it.

Dibs comes in

Ah, Dibs, come and sit down, Mr Walker's just going to tell us how he seduced one of the job lots. And then we'll give him the old heave-ho; poor chap's hopelessly young for early retirement, it'll have to be a straight sacking.

Dibs Oh dear, I'm awfully sorry Mr Walker.

Walker But ... but I mean I didn't think that er ... this ... was a sacking issue.

Prin Not automatically, Mr Walker. Not automatically. One enjoys considerable latitude. Depends partly on how good a story you make out of it. Come on then.

Walker hesitates

Dibs Prin, I don't think it's a good idea for me to be here. Perhaps if the Head of English were to ...

Prin Don't be silly, Dibs. Need your disinterested counsel as Vice-Principal. Value it. Mr Walker needs you as prisoner's friend. She'll be a lot more sympathetic than me, Mr Walker. She'll probably plead your cause for you. Head of English? Gladys Carp may be a world authority on Mrs Molesworth but she's not the woman for this sort of caper. Sit tight Dibs. Fire away Mr Walker.

Walker (*tongue-tied*) Well ... there isn't really anything to say. It well, you know. It just happened. And then went on happening.

Pause

Prin You'll have to do better than that, you know. You may favour this minimalist school, but it doesn't go down at all well with us, does it, Dibs? Detail detail and plenty of it.

Walker I'd rather not give her name, Principal.

Prin No, all right, but do get on.

Walker Well, um . . . as I said at my interview, if you remember . . . I try to teach literature in a non-authoritarian style. I think we should be open to their responses. I see the teacher as facilitator and resource . . . putting the materials directly into the hands of the students.

Dibs suppresses a chortle. Prin gives her a look

Prin Don't mind her Mr Walker. But I hope this isn't all going to stay on the theoretical level.

Walker I didn't find her particularly attractive at first. She was reticent in group discussions, tended to stare at me with a sort of glum ferocity I took for extreme boredom. So naturally, I wasn't much disposed in her favour. Then she asked to see me to discuss a difficulty she said she was experiencing with structuralist poetics. When she came to my room, she sat very close. I er, assumed that this was the result of faulty social learning, and soldiered on with my explanation, trying to move tactfully backwards, so that we weren't in such . . . uncomfortable proximity. My room is very small. Very warm, too. I've never been able to get the radiator to turn off.

Dibs We'll put that in hand immediately, Mr Walker.

Prin If he's staying. On.

Walker What I suppose I'm saying is that it felt too warm, we were too close, I couldn't stop looking at the little beads of sweat on her upper lip, and I was beginning to feel a little dizzy and I paused. She said something about being able to understand it when I was telling her, but that when she was on her own it all fell apart, but it wasn't what she said, it was her breath on my face, she was as close as that, her breath was warm and sweet, it was like the rush of hot air when you open the oven door. Anyway, I managed to say something about getting a bit of fresh air. It was all I could think of. And we walked across the playing fields. There were a lot of crows and magpies walking about slowly on the grass, looking as if they had their hands behind their backs. I remember thinking that's odd, I didn't realize they got on together, crows and magpies. And she was talking about what it felt like to be a PE thickie, as she put it, on a Mickey Mouse degree, as she put it, and how she felt such a lot but she couldn't find the words to say it in, she had all these thoughts but no words, and I said Saussure and Terry Eagleton wouldn't think much of that, but John Donne and I would go along with it, and I very much wanted to help her find her true voice . . . anyway, we'd reached the woods by then, and she gave me a rather odd look, and said: "Lie down, Mr Walker, and shut your eyes. Little experiment. It won't hurt." (*He pauses*) At first I thought it was the tips of her fingers she'd placed gently on my eyelids, one by one . . . and then she said: you can open your eyes now. And of course it wasn't her fingertips.

Pause

Prin I see now. You're making a complaint of sexual harassment, Mr

Walker! Bit novel, it's usually the other way round, but I like the audacity of it. What shall we do, Dibs, set up a little Faculty Board working party on it?

Walker No, no! I'm not complaining. I found it . . . extraordinarily moving.

Prin Well, yes, you would, wouldn't you?

Dibs I think it's rather moving, Prin.

Prin There you are, Mr Walker.

Walker (*to Dibs*) Thank you.

Prin Well, get on then.

Walker Um . . . we made love there and then. Without saying anything else. It was very strange. It was like learning a new language.

Prin Should have thought you were fairly fluent in that language, Mr Walker. D'you think he's pulling our legs, Dibs?

Walker No, I'm not honestly. It's just very hard to express. It was *her* language, you see. Her unique idiolect. She'd found her voice. And she was using me . . . using my body . . . to talk with. So it wasn't simply like learning a language. I was part of the language she was speaking.

Dibs (*fervently*) ". . . one might almost say, her body thought." Sorry.

Walker (*to Dibs, acknowledging the quote*) Yes. And since then, I haven't been able to get enough of her.

Prin Well, Mr Walker. You seem to have been having a bloody good time.

Walker (*involuntary laugh*) Yes I have. (*The laugh again*) Yes I feel wonderful. It's ridiculous. (*The laugh again*) I'm sorry. I'm sorry. It's just all this seems so unreal. (*Determinedly he stifles another laugh*) I'm sorry.

Prin Mr Walker. I'm getting a very odd feeling about all this. I think it *is* unreal. I'm beginning to suspect you've made the whole thing up. You don't get your sexual pleasure from affairs with students, you get it from recounting sexual fantasies to middle-aged gentlewomen. That's it, isn't it? You're a flasher by narrative, aren't you?

Walker No, no, really. Every word is true.

Prin Then I have to ask you. Mr Walker, what can possibly be your motive for coming here and telling us all about it? Why couldn't you be discreet about it?

Walker Oh, that's easy. She's pregnant, you see, and her father's threatened to make a lot of trouble for me. Thought I ought to get my confession in first.

Prin Ah. I see. Very prudent of you. Disappointingly job-lottish, but sensible. So her father's going to make trouble for you, is he?

Walker Yes he is.

Prin Wrong. Nobody's going to make trouble for you, not at this college, unless I choose to make trouble for you.

Walker He, er, talked a lot about his power and influence.

Prin He did, did he? Well, it was empty talk, Mr Walker, whoever he is. No-one has power and influence over me. Except my loved ones. I, however, have a great deal of power over you. Don't I?

Walker Yes.

Prin Yes.

Walker Er, what are you going to do, Principal?

Prin Haven't decided yet. I'll probably do it on a whim. Couple of things I'd like you to think about Mr Walker. I *was* quite impressed by your pedagogic theory, lecturer as resource, vocabulary of the body, all that. But it's simply not on in the present economic climate. We're working on a twelve to one staff–student ratio here, you can't teach them all that way, there simply aren't enough hours in the day. Not to mention other limiting factors. Which brings me to my second point. You've an inadequate imagination, Mr Walker. I advise you to cultivate it. Imagination, properly cultivated, can transcend the messiness of life. All that bother, Mr Walker. All that expense of spirit. And that John Thomas of yours, fluent as he is in foreign languages, will one day, not so very far away, stutter and falter into an embarrassed silence. And where will you be then, Mr Walker?

Walker Well, I . . .

Prin That was a rhetorical question. Take yourself off now, there's a good chap.

Walker (*rising*) Er, right. Thank you. (*To Dibs, with feeling*) Thank you.

Walker exits

Prin Well, what shall we do with him, Dibs? Shall we bounce him out, just for the hell of it, or let him stay and carry on the good work?

Dibs You can be very callous, can't you?

Prin Not with everyone. (*After a pause*) You seem to have a soft spot for little Dick Wanker.

Dibs He's a nice man, I think, Prin. He's not a very good man, and he doesn't seem very strong, and I don't think he has much integrity. But he is rather nice.

Prin He's not a sweaty Camembert, I'll give you that. He'll never amount to anything, of course. All right. Just for you—we'll keep him as a sort of pet. All right?

Dibs Well. I think there's something you ought to know first.

Prin What?

Dibs I'm not surprised he was shy about telling you the name of the student.

Prin Not Oninka Small?

Dibs Melanie Kite.

Prin Never heard of her.

Dibs Yes, you have.

Prin Have I? Melanie Kite. No relation of the Viable Package, surely?

Dibs His daughter.

Prin Ah.

Dibs Don't you remember? We agreed to accept her as a favour to him, her A level grades were distinctly iffy, school report very mediocre, all they could suggest was that she might be a very late developer.

Prin Well, they were right there. John Kite's daughter, eh? Yes, I do vaguely remember something about it. Why don't I know her?

Dibs Because she's a very mediocre second year dance major, you know you never take an interest till they're in the third year, and then only in a special few.

Prin Yes, Dibs. I do know that. Oh, my goodness me, I do know that. Everyone stop, I said. Watch Dorothy move.

She looks at Dibs now. It's the look we saw before. They hold the look for a moment, then Dibs moves uncomfortably

Dibs Look, Prin.

Prin And now I'm going to make an exception for little Miss Kite. Dig her out for me, would you Dibs, and get her over here now?

Dibs She'll be in the dance studio.

Prin Excellent. Haul her out. Catch her in mid-flight, tuck her under your arm squawking and flapping, and trot her straight in here.

Dibs But you're seeing her father in a minute.

Prin So I am. What a bore. Odd how one forgets the insignificant. "Hallo, Peggy, thought we ought to have a quickie on the agenda, lay down a little game plan for the big match, eh?" What a noodle that man is.

Dibs He's probably got a very viable package worked out, for the merger. Don't underestimate him, will you Prin?

Prin Little Dibs, little Dibs. You're here to comfort and sustain me, not to advise me on policy. All that is necessary is that Kite should not underestimate me, and he's learnt that over the years. Still, you're right. Two Kites at once, flapping and pecking all over the place, bit much. Hold the daughter in readiness and loose her to me when the father leaves. All right?

Dibs Yes. All right. Prin, do be careful.

Prin He's only the Director of Education, Dibs. He's not the Big Bad Wolf.

Dibs No. That part was bagged a long time ago, wasn't it?

Dibs goes out

Prin goes over and lifts the phone

Prin Has Mr Kite arrived? ... Splendid ... Yes, of course straight away. (*She replaces the receiver*)

Kite comes in. A powerful-looking chap in his late forties. He comes at her with his hand ready to shake

Kite Peggy. Good to see you again.

Prin Good-morning, Mr Kite.

Kite I do wish you'd learn to call me John you know.

Prin I rather wish you'd learn not to call me Peggy, Mr Kite. Still: one can't expect to have all one's wishes granted in this world, can one?

Kite No. Absolutely.

Prin Unfortunately. Do sit down, then.

He does

Kite Shame about lunch. Still, I, ah, thought we should have a quickie about this afternoon's meeting.

Prin Yes, I did think you might have that in mind.

Kite It could, ah, it could turn out to be the crucial one, Peggy. Doesn't have to be, but I think everyone's ready to take the package on board and row it in.

Prin And what package would that be, Mr Kite?

Kite Well I think it's a very viable package, Peggy.

Prin Oh good. We do like our packages to be viable, don't we?

Kite Yes we do. I see the Poly as the best bet, they're very ready to close. You've got your flexibility with the Poly. Tremendous technical backup, you'll be able to expand massively on the Science Education side, and there's solid funding from the M.S.C. earmarked. Earmarked specifically.

Prin We do like our earmarks specific.

Kite I think it adds up.

Prin And, of course, they want to get their greedy paws on our grounds and cover them with muddied oafs.

Kite Don't think a them and us attitude is very helpful at this stage, Peggy. Hedley Stafford at the Poly has been very flexible. And of course they're going to want something.

Prin And of course the funding will stay within your area.

Kite We've always worked well together in the past. I like to feel that we've got pretty close, you and I.

Prin We're a viable package, are we?

Kite I like to think so, Peggy. Of course there is the University.

Prin But if we merged with them you'd lose your control of funding, wouldn't you?

Kite Can't draw the wool over your eyes, Peggy. I think that the great thing about the University offer is the lever it gives us on the Poly. Hedley Stafford won't be difficult because he knows it could go the other way. D'you know, I think we could sew it all up this afternoon.

Prin I see. So the, let me get this right, the game plan is to take it on board, sew it all up, and row it in!

Kite As a viable package, yes. In a way it's a good thing you won't be present this afternoon: means I'll be able to foreground your personal position.

Prin You'll foreground my position in my absence.

Kite Confidentially I think it's best. It'll be plain sailing. (*He lowers his voice*) Deputy Director of the Polytechnic. Or if it goes the other way, a personal Chair at the University is definitely on the cards.

Prin What treats!

Kite Thought you'd be pleased.

Prin You thought I'd be pleased, did you? What on earth could make you think I'd be pleased with being a token professor in a third-rate provincial degree factory? My dear man, I could have had a chair at Oxford University, but I had other purposes in life. And they certainly didn't and don't include being Deputy Director under a bland and mediocre nonentity like Hedley Stafford. You're dealing with a prima donna here, you know.

Kite Yes, I did realize that.

Prin Well let's have no more of this nonsense. What I am, and what I shall continue to be, is the Principal of this college. It may seem an eccentric choice to you, but that's how I like it.

Kite Not on, Peggy, I'm afraid. I know just how you feel, but you see if you were still called Principal it wouldn't look like a proper merger, it would imply that the College still existed as an independent entity.

Prin Quite.

A pause while this sinks in

Kite Oh, no. Oh, no. The Poly wouldn't wear it. Nor would the University.

Prin Then that would seem to be their problem.

Kite Yours too, Peggy, I'm afraid.

Prin Kite I'm getting frightfully bored with all this. Just tell them there isn't going to be any merger, and row the whole thing away. Sew it up, tie bricks to it, and drop it overboard, and everyone will feel *much* better. Now what's all this I hear about your threatening my lecturers?

Kite Ah. That. You've seen the man then.

Prin This very morning, Mr Kite. I needn't tell you I was very shocked.

Kite Well I'm glad you find it shocking. I find it shocking. I think it's bloody monstrous. He's got to go, of course. Now I'm not a vindictive man as you know Peggy I'm quite happy to have it processed as a voluntary redundancy. Must say I'd hoped for something better from this college, I'm extremely disappointed Peggy.

Prin Oh, I don't think you should be. Your very mediocre daughter, whom we accepted, I believe, out of compassion and against our better judgement, your daughter's enjoyed a quite disproportionate amount of contact time with the English staff. In the matter of individual tutorials, young Mr Walker has gone quite beyond the call of duty.

Kite I'll say he has! He's been bloody shafting her! The little sod's got her pregnant! (*Emotional stress has brought out a lurking Midlands accent as well as a latent vocabulary*) Christ. That's my little girl we're talking about. I've changed that girl's nappies. I taught that girl to swim. I ... I love that girl.

Prin I do understand your feelings, Mr Kite. But I must correct you. She's not your little girl. She's a young woman now, and she belongs to herself. And I'm sure you do love her, but it seems she prefers to be shafted by Mr Walker.

Kite is speechless for a moment. Mingled rage and incredulity

Kite You ... you just don't care what you say or do, do you? You don't care about anything.

Prin Oh. I do care, you know. And I take my games very seriously.

Kite There's just no dealing with you, is there?

Prin It would seem not.

Kite You'll regret this, Peggy.

He goes out

A flurry of growling off

(*Off*) Bloody dog!

Prin And now he'll huff and he'll puff ... Oh, Prin. Unwise. But fun.

Dibs comes in looking a bit flustered

Dibs What have you done to the Director of Education?

Prin I haven't done anything to him. We had a full and frank exchange of views, that's all. Franker on my side than on his I fancy. Still, he did confess to an incestuous passion for that daughter of his. Dreadful man. Dreadful. Never mind. Where is she, Dibs?

Dibs Oh she's gone. Dragged her off to give her a piece of his mind. I think.

Prin Well, that shouldn't take very long. I'll see her after lunch. Lunch. Yes. I must be delaying you, Dibs. You'll be wanting to get away to Dr Bile and his newt cutlets.

Dibs Well, I s'pose really I ought to be ... look, if you like, I'll put it off.

Prin Wouldn't dream of it.

Dibs Really?

Prin Wouldn't dream of it. I shall go into Hall, Dibs. I shall lunch at High Table. And afterwards harangue punters.

Dibs Prin. Don't ... I mean, try not to go over the top. It's so bad for recruitment.

Prin We're interested in quality here, not quantity. Off you go to your frog spawn, little Dibs. I shall be the soul of tact.

Dibs hesitates, then goes off

Prin comes forward

(*To the audience*) It's very gratifying to see you here in such large numbers at our Open Day. We like to offer prospective students, and the parents of prospective students, the opportunity of seeing and experiencing what we are about here. I am the Principal of this college. That's Principal with an A L at the end, not an L E. I say this because when it is time for you to make your applications, the more illiterate amongst you will favour the latter spelling. Those applications will of course go straight into the waste-paper basket. However, they do unconsciously reveal a certain truth. I do embody a principle. That principle is the pursuit of excellence. It's quite unfamiliar to most of you of course. I fully realize that you're leading lives of quite mind-numbing mediocrity, using perhaps a tenth or a twentieth of the human potential you were born with. And you feel guilty about that, of course, and resentful that you're being reminded of it. It's in the interest of the system that you should feel like that, and stay in that benighted state. I am interested in transforming society. My graduates bloom like terrifying exotic flowers in classrooms all over the country, showing the children how to be extraordinary, as I have shown them to be extraordinary. The power for extraordinary change exists in every human being. Think what it could be like to allow yourselves to be wholly known. Well: I shan't take up any more of my valuable time. I have people to bully. I have plots to put down. Try to understand the essence of this place. It's not an ordinary place. And then, perhaps, I shall meet some of you next year as first-year students, when I shall take great pleasure in terrifying the wits out of you and changing your lives. Good-afternoon. (*She turns her back and walks upstage*)

The Lights fade

CURTAIN

ACT II

The table with cloth and flowers is set up downstage as for the Academic Board scene. Prin sits C, Dibs on one side, Boyle on the other

Prin Well, I'm surprised to see that so many of you have turned up to the Examination Board this afternoon. You must be expecting some sort of treat. Perhaps we should think of charging admission fees, boost the flower fund, buy Dr Bile a few more *rats* to rip up with his little scalpel, eh?

Boyle chuckles good-humouredly: Dibs feels queasy

Boyle (*through the chuckle*) Er, Boyle, Principal.

Prin And all we have to do really is ratify the results of the Final Teaching Practice. We'll whiz through that at a fairly brisk pace if you don't mind, as you know, I have a very low boredom threshold and the good doctor has another meeting to attend.

Dibs (*referring to notes; her public manner is lively and ingratiating*) Well, it's been a very good year, really. Professor McKechnie, the External Examiner, commented favourably on the general high level of ambition, idealism and flair which he saw in the more able students. However—he wondered whether the more mediocre students, who are after all the backbone of the profession, could have received more attention and encouragement. I, er, took the liberty of putting it to Professor McKechnie that perhaps we shouldn't be seen to be encouraging mediocrity all that much . . .

Prin Good for you! Charlie McKechnie was ever a plodder. Last time we invite *him*! Right. Failures, retakes, fled the country, problem cases please, Vice-Principal.

Dibs Miss Dobbs, sadly, was in tears for practically the whole of her practice at South Street High.

Prin Well knowing the conditions they operate under at South Street, one can hardly blame the poor girl. I take it we're giving her another go? Somewhere a bit less terrifying?

Dibs Well, not immediately. She's hospitalized at the moment.

Prin All right, keep it under review. On.

Dibs (*referring to notes*) Miss Nokes withdrew after the unfortunate events at All Saints comprehensive.

Prin Unfortunate events?

Dibs Er, trampoline party, Principal.

Prin Ah, yes, pity. Promising girl, I always thought.

Dibs But she's doing awfully well as trainee play-leader on Eighteen-Thirty holidays. Er . . . Miss Muttley failed to complete the requisite number of days, after a lively and eventful start to her school practice. She, er, claimed to be leading a small expedition to view Crusader castles in Syria.

Prin Tricky. How small was the expedition.

Dibs Well, very small, really, Principal. Miss Muttley, her motor bike, and one of her fifth-form pupils.

Prin We'll recommend a retake, if she ever gets back. Got a lot of time for Muttley. Agreed?

Boyle Well, no Principal, with respect I think this needs more detailed——

Prin Fine, fine, we'll make it Chairman's action, no discussion required. Retake for Muttley. Any more, Dibs?

Dibs No, that's the lot.

Prin Science Education?

Boyle Eighty-four candidates, eighty-four passes, Principal.

Prin No distinctions?

Boyle We prefer to process teaching practice on a pass fail basis. Principal, in the Science Education Department. And we work to very rigorous standards.

Prin How very dull. How one wishes that one day a person of excellence would emerge from those swirling fumes. However. On, on. Distinctions?

Dibs All in PE and Dance. Maggie Savage, Oninka Small, and Julie Cinnamon.

Prin And they work to rigorous standards too, Dr Boyle. Maggie Savage, Oninka Small, and Julie Cinnamon. What a luminous trinity to unleash upon the world. Well, let's sign the lists.

Boyle Just a minute, Principal. Like to raise a query about Miss Cinnamon's distinction.

Prin *You'd* like to raise a query about Julie *Cinnamon*?

Boyle Yes. Principal, I was supervising a student in the same school, took the opportunity of observing Miss Cinnamon's science, didn't detect any distinction quality there.

Prin Well, you wouldn't, would you.

Boyle One of the pupils had brought in a dead fieldmouse. I expected Miss Cinnamon to take this opportunity to introduce her class to some scientific investigation of a properly rigorous kind. She did not. After the lesson I suggested that she'd missed an opportunity for dissection. She said she preferred to investigate the living world while it was still alive. I asked her what she did propose to do with the fieldmouse, and she said she was planning a fertility ritual along multi-ethnic lines, and that I could come and wail along with the rest if I liked. I declined this invitation and judged her attitude to science to be frivolous and irresponsible. However, as I knew she was being proposed for a distinction, I requested permission to observe a lesson in her main subject. She said that she didn't allow voyeurs, as she put it, but I could come as a participant if I fancied it. The lesson was fifth-year dance. There was no written lesson plan: I formed the conclusion that Miss Cinnamon was working intuitively off the top of her head for much of the time. There was a great deal of rapid and in my opinion potentially dangerous activity. There was also a great deal of laughter, much of it directed at myself. The ah, the floor was rather slippery, and I found some difficulty in keeping my footing. In the absence of declared and quantifiable objectives I found it difficult to grasp what Miss Cinnamon was aiming at. It was not, to put it mildly, my idea of excellence. However, in fairness to Miss Cinnamon, I should say that her manner throughout was poised and confident, that there was what I suppose you'd call a sort of stylishness to the whole performance, and that once or twice in the latter stages of the lesson I thought I did catch the occasional glimpse of A-ness.

Dibs turns her head sharply. Prin more slowly

Prin Glimpse of *what*?
Boyle A-ness, Principal. Distinction quality.
Prin Oh. I see. Giggling *again*, Mr Hoole? Well. All that seems very satisfactory. You're a lucky man, Dr Boyle. Not everyone is granted these occasional glimpses. (*Her eyes briefly rake the audience*) I take it that the Examination Board ratifies Miss Cinnamon's distinction? Good. (*She signs the list. As she does so:*)
Boyle What did the external examiner say?
Prin I've signed the list, Dr Boyle. It's all over. It's history now. Thank you all very much. (*To Boyle*) Enjoyed that immensely.

Prin goes upstage and off

Boyle shoves papers savagely into his briefcase

Boyle (*bitterly*) She's a character.
Dibs She's a bit difficult today.
Boyle When was she ever any different?
Dibs It's hard to explain, John. You only see her when she's ... putting herself about. She can be quite extraordinarily nice. I think she's a bit frightened of you.
Boyle She's frightened of me? I had this teacher once. In junior school. Miss Foster her name was. She wore a sort of leather flying helmet, indoors and out, summer and winter. Suppose she was bald or something. She should have been a figure of fun, but she wasn't. She had this way of looking at me that said quite clearly that nothing I could ever say or do would ever satisfy her. She had her favourites too. And I used to try so hard. I used to want to say, look at me, Miss Foster, I've done six pages, I've got all my sums right, what else do I have to do? My face didn't fit, though, somehow. I even went back there, once. She was dead by then, of course. I went into the classroom. Room Four. She always had Room Four. It felt exactly the same. Everyone knows I run a damn good department.
Dibs John. Don't. You're *winning*.
Boyle At least she got my name right. Miss Foster I mean.
Dibs Oh John. It's just a joke, Prin getting your name wrong. It doesn't mean anything.
Boyle Yes it does. It's a way of expressing her contempt for me. I told her it didn't particularly bother me, that's not the truth. It does, it does particularly bother me. Her contempt bothers me. I try to feel contempt

for her, but I don't feel contempt for her. I stand in bloody awe of the malevolent old bitch. I respect her bloody intellect. That book she wrote, all right, it's twenty years out of date, nobody uses it as a text book any more except this place, but it was stunningly original for its time, it did the fundamental thinking for a philosophy of physical education, and it wasn't even her bloody subject discipline! She'll always be remembered for that book you know.

Dibs And other things.

Boyle I publish, my research profile's all right, my stuff's respected in the field.

Dibs I know, John.

Boyle But it's not stunningly original. And hers is. Was. I bloody admire her, and she pisses all over me. Excuse me. Shouldn't have said that.

Dibs It's all right. She does arouse strong feelings.

Boyle I'll say she does. Well. She won't be doing it much longer, will she? Not to me she won't.

Dibs No.

Boyle She isn't even going to attend the bloody meeting. How's that for arrogance?

Dibs It isn't really arrogance. Well, it isn't just arrogance. I think she knows what's going to happen.

Boyle Well, it can't happen too soon for me. Sooner she's out of here the better for all of us. There just isn't room for her sort any more.

Dibs Her sort? What on earth do you mean, her sort? You don't know the first thing about her, do you? I don't think you know the first thing about me sometimes.

Boyle I don't know how you've put up with her bullying all these years. I don't know that about you.

Dibs Because it hasn't just been bullying—because it isn't really bullying anyway, it's just that that's the only way she—it's just that she can't ... It's because I love her of course. Oh, go to your stupid meeting!

Dibs goes off

Boyle stares after her as the table clears, then exits

Prin comes into her office, sits in a chair

Dibs comes in

Prin Hallo.

Dibs Are you all right?

Pause

Prin There was a lot of hope around, thirty years ago. Did you notice that? Really quite a lot of hope.

Dibs Well, I was just a little girl then.

Prin Just a little Dorothy bag.

Dibs No, not a little Dorothy bag. I was a little Dot in those days. That's what my best friend called me. She was Squib and I was Dot and she was the best at headstands in the whole school and I was the best at cartwheels. And we both had our hair in plaits because we both wanted to be the same. And yes, we were full of hopes. And people were full of hopes for us too. And everybody liked us, me and Squib, all the other girls and the teachers and everyone, because we weren't just good at headstands and cartwheels, we were really, I think, we really must have been, very nice girls.

Prin Yes, I should think you probably were very nice girls. I should like to have known you then.

Dibs I wonder if I'd like to have known you, thirty years ago.

Prin I doubt it. I was less of a sentimentalist then. More of an intellectual. Though rather more naïve than I should have been, I fear. Let me put you in the picture, Dibs ... Thirty years ago practically everyone in the world was a privately educated left-wing Oxford historian, and we were all absolutely choking with hope, and we all set out to change the world. The quaint notion entertained by all of us was that we could change the world through education. Bit too much of a hard slog for most of them of course. They fancied something a little more chic, like spying for Russia. Silly old queens. Or they sold out to our local bunch of crooks in one boring way or another. Actually Blunt tried to recruit *me* once, did I ever mention that?

Dibs Yes, you did, Prin.

Prin I told him I couldn't possibly be doing with all those microdots. I sent him packing.

Dibs Heard it.

Prin Well you're hearing it again then. Where have they all gone now? It was us who stayed. Us dikes. Do you know, in thirty years, not one single person has worked up the courage to ask me about my sexual life?

Dibs They talk about it behind your back.

Prin That is as I would wish. God, Dibs I get so sick of this place sometimes, apart from a few bright stars it's such a swamp of mediocrity, full of frightened little second-raters, stumbling round terrified out of their wits without the faintest idea what's going on. Walker, Boyle, Kite. Never mind. Four more days, Dibs, and we can shake them off our sensible shoes. Two weeks to ourselves in the cottage, and then Greece! Tee hee, said Tiger Tim!

Dibs Look. Prin. This is going to be difficult to say.

Prin I don't want to hear anything difficult. Save it for the cottage. Save it for Greece. Things sound better in Greece. Even difficult things.

Dibs Well, that's the point, in a way.

Prin How did your *lunch* go? Roast rat, was it? Grey squirrel, perhaps? I've heard that Bile is fond of ferret. I imagine him sitting up in bed in brown and yellow striped pyjamas, masticating juicily in time with a Sousa March, with a ferret's foot dangling from the corner of his little thin-lipped muzzle. He hums to himself as with his free hand he turns the pages. Ferret juice runs down his chin, and on to the glossy illustrated pages. Yum yum yum, he murmurs. Two hundred plates in full colour. And what do they depict? Need you ask? The splayed genitalia——

Dibs Oh, for Christ's sake give it a rest!

Short pause

Prin I'm sorry.

Long pause. Dibs's outburst has made her go all shaky

Dibs We had sausage rolls. Made with ordinary pork sausage. We had
lettuce. We had tomatoes. We drank white wine. And yes, I'm quite sure it
wasn't rat urine. It was Yugoslav Riesling.

Prin Damned close-run thing then.

Dibs Oh, you're so clever aren't you?

Prin Yes, indeed, little pig.

Dibs And it was all actually quite pleasant. A bit on the boring side, but
sometimes a bit of boredom can seem quite nice. And Kite turned up a bit
later on, and actually he was quite pleasant too. In point of fact.

Prin In point of what?

Dibs In point of fact, Prin, that's how we do tend to go on in Science
Education, and it's quite comfy rolling the old clichés back and forth, it
makes a bit of a change, you can send your mind for a nice little trip
around the garden, and when it comes back they're all still there,
nothing's changed, we're all still sewing it up and rowing it in and coming
back to each other on that one, it can actually grow on you.

Prin Like scabies, yes.

Dibs And John Boyle isn't actually a monster, he's a rather ordinary but
quite harmless human being, as most of us tend to be in point of fact. You
think people are figments of your imagination, but we're not. We're real.
We're all real.

Pause

Prin Little Dibs, little Dibs. Who has been feeding you this dangerous
nonsense?

Dibs I'm not coming on holiday with you this year.

Prin turns her head slowly and dangerously. But Dibs is now looking at . . .

   Melanie Kite, who has just come in rather awkwardly and hesitantly

Hallo.

Melanie Sorry . . . there wasn't anyone in the office. So I just sort of came in.

Prin So you did.

Melanie Um . . . you wanted to see me.

Prin Did I? Who are you?

Dibs She's Melanie Kite.

Melanie I'm Melanie Kite.

Prin Oh. Yes, I did want to see you. I see what they mean about the glum
ferocity, don't you Dibs?

Dibs I think it's just shyness, Prin.

Prin Haven't I met you before?

Melanie Don't think so. Not really. Only, you know, when you talked to us
all. Be extraordinary, all that.

Prin Oh, don't worry about it. You're probably something out of Spiritus Mundi, slouching towards Bethlehem to be born.

Melanie Sorry?

Prin Are you not a student of English Literature?

Melanie Only subsid.

Prin Yes. Well, Miss Kite. So you're the one who's been putting the future of the college at risk.

Melanie Have I?

Prin By assaulting lecturers.

Melanie Didn't *assault* any of them.

Prin I understand that you did, Miss Kite. I understand—do sit down by the way, Miss Kite.

Melanie's looking a bit alarmed

Dibs It's all right, Melanie.

Melanie sits on the chair by the desk

Prin My understanding is that you cornered your English tutor in his small and overheated office, breathed on him oppressively, then took him to the woods and indecently assaulted him.

Melanie stares at her

There were magpies and crows about at the time, does that refresh your memory?

Melanie Did Dick Walker tell you that?

Prin More or less, more or less. You're denying it, are you?

Melanie Well, it wasn't really like that.

Prin Excellent! You have a different story. The Vice-Principal and I will be delighted to hear it.

Melanie Oh. No. It doesn't matter. I mean it all sort of comes to the same thing. Doesn't matter how it happened, does it, I mean we have been f— ... we have been ... having a relationship.

Prin We're not mechanical engineers, Miss Kite. We're not interested in blocks and tackles, we're interested in the nature of perceived reality here!

Melanie (*to Dibs*) I don't know what she means. I don't know what she wants me to do.

Dibs Just tell her your version, Melanie. You'll be sympathetically listened to. We want to help you, Melanie.

Melanie (*with a wry smile*) That's what he said. Oh, all right then. I'd seen him, you know, looking at me in seminars. Quite a few of you do that. Not just the men lecturers either. I often wondered, you know, if people realize how much they give themselves away. He'd even sort of tail off in the middle of sentences, sometimes. And now and then, when it was boring, or I couldn't understand what was going on, I'd sort of wonder what it would be like to pull him. You know how you do. Oh, sorry. Didn't mean *you personally*. Not very good at expressing myself.

Prin And women over fifty years old, of course, have no sexuality at all. Quite, quite. Go on.

Melanie Well eventually after one of these seminars he stopped me going out and said he'd like a private word with me in his room. I thought, hallo, what's this then. Yes, it was hot in there. Didn't think I was breathing on him, specially. I felt a bit big for the room, you know what I mean? Anyway he said some stuff about how he was worried about how I didn't participate in the discussions, was anything bothering me, did I have any problems, he really wanted me to get the most out of the course, all that. He had this little bit of Blu-tack he kept fiddling about with, he'd given up smoking. Anyone could see what was on his mind. Anyway, I said the only problem I had was not being very good at English, or anything else, come to that, and then we were into oh I'm sure that's not the case it's just a matter of learning to find your own voice and articulate the what was it contradictions inherent in the life situation. Blu-tack going like mad by now, right? He'd sneak a look at me every now and then, see how it was going. I thought it was nice the way he was so shy and roundabout, I mean he could have just leapt on me. He was all sweating and fiddly and nervous, and there I was just sitting there like a big lump. Everyone has problems Melanie, he said, and then of course he went straight on and told me about his. He's got an identity crisis. Well, I expect you'd know about that. And then he went on about the terrible difficulties he was experiencing trying to be spontaneous and autonomous in an arena fraught with political contradictions relating to gender. I committed that one to memory.

Prin As well you might.

Melanie Turned out he was talking about teaching literature to an all-girls group. I thought it's not that, though really, is it, and of course it wasn't. Well it was only part of it. He's not getting on very well with his wife, you see. She's gone off sex since she had the babies. He doesn't blame her, but it makes him feel insensitive and incompetent and uncaring and bloody frustrated, well that's easy enough to understand. Blu-tack, Blu-tack, Blu-tack. Very pink in the face by now. So you see, Melanie, he said, I've got my problems too. And I was just thinking, all you need really is a good fuck, I was sitting there like a big lump thinking it, which of course was exactly what he wanted me to think. I'm such a pushover, really, it's a disgrace. Blu-tack, Blu-tack. He looks up, he looks down. Big innocent eyes. D'you ever say something and you think hallo, who said that? I heard myself saying, all you really need is a good fuck, Dick . . . Long pause, right?

Dibs Blu-tack, Blu-tack.

Melanie That's right. Well, that was it really.

Prin He invited you to go for a walk.

Melanie No, no. That was another time. No, the first time, we did it there. In his room.

Prin On the floor? In his office?

Melanie Well, eventually on the floor. We, er, we started off standing up sort of thing.

Prin I see.

Melanie I'm not complaining. It was all right, really, in his room. He's got

all these interesting posters to look at, on the wall and that. And you
know that glass panel over the doors, he'd tacked a poster over that too,
he must have borrowed some steps to do that, he's not that tall. He must
have been worried that one of his colleagues would get the steps and set
them up on the outside and climb up and look through the glass, I s'pose.
I didn't like to ask him at the time. I didn't feel I knew him well enough.

Prin Never mind that. That's immaterial.

Melanie Well I dunno what you want me to say! I never know what anyone
wants me to say!

Prin The wood! The crows and the magpies! I want to hear about the
language of the body!

Melanie I told you. That was another time. He must have been intertextualising.

Prin He must have been what?

Melanie Intertextualising, you know. It's one of his words that, he does *talk*
to me you know. Well he did.

Prin I think you're wasting my time, Miss Kite.

Melanie Well I didn't ask to come. Why don't you lay off me? Know you're
going to chuck me out anyway. Why don't you just... get on with it?

Prin I know where I've seen you before. I've seen your photograph. Haven't
I?

Melanie Oh. Yeah. That.

Prin You're a very versatile young woman, aren't you?

Melanie That's one way of putting it.

Prin How would you put it?

Melanie I just do anything anyone asks me to.

Prin People must find you extremely useful, my dear.

Melanie S'pose they do. (*She looks down, then straight at Prin*) They call me
the college bicycle.

Pause

Prin (*gently*) Bicycles don't inspire love. You inspire love. That's not a
negligible thing. It's not everything, but it's not negligible. I tend on the
whole not to inspire love. Terror and loathing's more the ticket, eh Dibs?

Dibs Not always.

Prin I believe my dog—our dog—is fond of me. But dogs see more than
people do. So you do anything anyone asks you to, do you? Tell me,
would you do something for me if I asked you to?

Dibs (*warning*) Prin.

Prin Would you?

Melanie Well, I dunno. I mean, I haven't really ... I don't know if I could.

Prin Oh, I think you could. You're a dance major, aren't you?

Melanie Yes.

Prin I want to see you move.

Melanie Oh.

Prin Now.

Melanie Here?

Prin Yes, here. We'll put some music on, and watch you move. That will be very nice.

Melanie I'm not much good, really. I'd be embarrassed. Oh, what d'you want me to do that for?

Dibs Because it's what she does. It's her little ploy. Movement is truth, you see. It helps her to see right into your little soul.

Prin Don't be bitter, Dibs. (*To Melanie*) That was how Miss Minns came to my attention, you see. I watched her move. And now I want to see you move.

Dibs I know why you're doing this.

Prin Oh, do shut up. Put the music on. What was on will do fine.

Dibs *Chopin?*

Prin You used to move to Chopin. You could move to anything. You were a very versatile young woman in your day. Everybody stop, I said. Watch Dorothy move. (*To Melanie*) Take your shoes off. And your wrap.

Melanie is wearing a denim skirt over a leotard. It's easy for her to step out of it and kick her shoes off

Good. Stand quite still. Shut your eyes. Find your point of stillness. Go into yourself.

Melanie stands solidly, her feet a foot apart, her arms hanging loose by her sides

Don't think about what you want to say to me. Let your body say it. (*She nods to Dibs*)

Dibs switches the tape on

Don't move until you really have to move.

The music starts. Melanie is standing quite still. Then her right arm starts to tremble a little. Then it stops trembling. Prin turns her head to look at Dibs, who looks uneasy. Then looks back at Melanie. Very slowly Melanie's right arm comes up across her chest, her hand clasping her left shoulder. Then her left arm, the same movement. Her body sways. Left. Then right, then left. She uses this movement to launch her, three steps diagonally downstage. Then stoops, her weight on one foot. She opens her eyes wide, looking out into the audience, her arms come down and outwards, her head comes up, she stands tall. All this time she's been with her back to Prin. Now she turns. Takes three strong steps upstage, straight towards Prin. Stands balanced and tall with her feet wide apart, her arms out from her body, palms turned to Prin, as if saying quite powerfully: here I am, then. This is me. She holds this quite still for a few moments. Then gradually, she starts to shake, just a little at first, then quite violently. Then her arms come up, as before, cradling her body. Her head goes down, still shaking, she starts to curl her body over. She ends up kneeling, her head pulled down over her legs. Dibs makes a move to go to her. Prin stops her

Melanie (*indistinctly*) I don't like this.

Prin What?

Dibs switches the music off

Melanie (*raising her head*) I don't like this. All this stuff. All your stuff. Be extraordinary. Be remarkable. I mean I took it all in. I had a go at it, didn't I? And look at me now. I'm all fucked up. College bike, right? Can't even . . . It's you. Way you go on at people. Dick Walker's all right, it's you. You're the one who makes me feel harrassed.

She is standing by now. She picks up her shoes and her skirt and walks out

Prin Well, Dibs, did you enjoy that? Did it take you down Memory Lane? Not in your class, of course, not really a prima donna, but quite interesting in her own way. Really very promising material.

Dibs You really take the biscuit, you do. Didn't you understand what she was saying to you?

Prin Of course I did. I am, after all, the author of the standard work on the interpretation of human movement. You're dealing with a monument of unageing intellect here, little Dibs! Little Miss Kite would hardly present me with any problems. Would she?

Dibs Your book's twenty years out of date now. Everyone knows that. We're the only college in the country that's still using it!

Prin I'll overlook that, Dibs. I do understand. You really mustn't be jealous of me. You know I can't resist teasing you. Such a little hothead this afternoon. "Shan't come to Greece with you, so there" poor old thing. *Where else have you got to go?*

Dibs Christ. You just don't understand anything, do you?

Dibs walks out angrily

Prin Yes, I think I do. Bright little girl, that, in her way. Education *is* harassment. That's why it's so unpopular.

Dibs reappears, still het up

Dibs Talking to ourselves now, are we? Walker's here. Do you want to see him?

Prin Yes. Yes. I think I do.

Dibs Right!

She goes again

Prin Oh dear, oh dear. Tears before bedtime.

Barking and growling outside. Walker comes in

Walker Think he's beginning to get used to me.

Prin Mr Walker. How very nice. I feel like a stiffener. Mr Walker, it's been a difficult day. Will you join me?

Walker Stiffener?

Prin Whisky, Mr Walker. I'm proposing that we pour a glass of whisky down our throats, are you with me?

Walker Oh. Yes. Thank you very much. Might as well. (*His odd laugh*)

Prin (*pouring a couple of large straight ones: putting a little extra in her own as a second thought*) Bit fanciful, that tale you told me this morning, wasn't it?

Walker S'pose it was, a bit. Doesn't really matter now though does it? (*He laughs again*) Oh Christ.

Prin Indeed it does, Mr Walker. It's crucial. (*Handing him the drink*) I've seriously misjudged you, Mr Walker. I can admit a mistake. I thought you lacked imagination. I was wrong. You turned a mundane episode into a tale of courtly love. We see what we feel to be there, Mr Walker, and what you felt to be there was quite remarkable. You're a creative artist.

Walker No, honestly, I'm not really.

Prin That's how I see you. Here's to you, Mr Walker, here's to us. We're two of a kind, you and I, I fancy.

Walker Are we?

Prin You just need to take things one stage further. With an imagination like yours, who needs the real world? All that mess, all those hydraulics. Bad enough being chained inside a dying animal without going looking for comic humiliations, eh?

Walker Er, yes, suppose so. (*The laugh again*) Oh, God. Sorry.

Prin Well, I've made my mind up. I'm going to keep you on.

Walker Sorry? I don't understand.

Prin Sounds simple enough to me. I'm not going to dismiss you, Mr Walker. You're far too valuable to lose for such a minor mishap of the sexual comedy.

Walker But I don't see ... I mean, it's final now, isn't it? I mean the Director of Education called me in after the meeting.

Prin Did he indeed? And?

Walker Said they were letting me go, he wasn't nasty about it, said he was going to make it as easy as he could, restructuring redundancy.

Prin He can't do that, Mr Walker. I'm the principal here, not Kite.

Walker I think he can, actually. I mean he does pay our salaries.

Prin That doesn't give him any right to dismiss his enemies.

Walker Well, um, (*laughing*) I think it does, really. Apparently it was a discussion of the full Governing Board.

Prin It was, was it? Well, we'll fight it, Mr Walker! We'll overturn it! These are little people, these are men with soft underbellies and tiny brains. They are all of them frightened of excellence! We'll make them jump!

Walker No, really, it's very kind of you, Principal, but I don't think it'll really do any good. I'm not *really* excellent, you know.

Prin Mr Walker. I appointed you, I only appoint extraordinary people.

Walker I'm not worth it, really. I really haven't the faintest idea what it's all about. Hardly anybody has. I've got a good vocabulary, I can say the things people want to hear. That's all. I just want people to like me. The D.o.E. Mr Kite was very decent. I cried a bit when he broke the news, don't know why, did the trick though. Said he'd find me a little opening at the Tech. Low-level stuff, you know. Teaching Life Skills for the Manpower Services Commission. Life Skills. I haven't got any Life Skills. But it's a job, isn't it? (*He laughs*) I screw his daughter and he gives me a job! (*Laughing*) Isn't it weird? I ... I think he likes me! (*He can't stop himself laughing*) I'm sorry. It's not funny! (*He laughs some more*) I'm sorry (*He stops*)

Prin Mr Walker, your laughter sounds to me remarkably like the laughter of despair.

Walker Yes, you're quite right. I'm actually staring disaster in the face, aren't I? (*He laughs*) I mean this Life Skills thing won't pay more than peanuts, I won't be able to keep the mortgage up, I've already ruined my wife's life, and I don't know what the fuck I'm going to do about Melanie. What did you think of her, did you like her?

Prin Quite an interesting girl, I thought.

Walker Yes, I think so. Don't know why. She's really thick, you know. She's only ever read one book right through. We've got nothing in common, nothing. I'm really crazy about her! (*He starts to laugh again*) You know my wife's a really wonderful person! I'm sorry! I'm sorry. (*He sobers right down*) I don't know what the fuck it's all about. I don't think anybody does now. (*A long pause. He gets up*) Um ... thanks for the stiffener. And, you know ... sorry. It isn't funny. I know that.

He goes

Prin Stiffener, stiffener, I need another stiffener. (*She gets herself one. She goes to the window*) Betty Brain ... Maggie Savage ... Melinda Peebles ... Oninka Small ... Julie Cinnamon. "Her pure and eloquent blood Spoke in her cheeks, and so distinctly wrought, That one might almost say, her body thought." And if you did, by golly, you'd be right.

Kite comes in

Thought you'd be back. You've cut it a bit fine little pig. Nearly missed the late afternoon parade.

Kite Hallo, Peggy.

Prin What a nasty surprise.

Kite I'd like to have a word. Like you to be the first to know.

Prin This is a rather precious time of day for me, Mr Kite, I trust you'll make it a quickie.

Kite Well I don't want to prolong it unduly. Bit difficult, this.

Prin Yes, I should imagine it is. But you'll manage it somehow, no doubt.

Kite Case of having to, Peggy.

Prin People are very cruel aren't they, compared with apes, or dogs? I wonder why we're like that. Why couldn't you have enacted a token mounting of poor little Mr Walker, instead of driving him out of the pack?

Kite Dick Walker's getting a very fair deal, all things considered. He's a bad lad. He gets exactly the same deal as the rest of them. My daughter's a bit of a problem case, I can see that as well as anyone. Don't see that that's any excuse for someone in a position of authority and trust to ... to ...

Prin To use her like the college bicycle?

Kite (*bitterly*) You've got a wonderful way with words, Peggy. Anyway, as I said, there was nothing vindictive about it. He was naturally in line for rationalization, and he's getting the same treatment as everybody else in his position.

Prin How many of my staff have been shafting your daughter then?

Kite Easy, Peggy. It's been a long day. I have my sensitivities. I'm talking about the other redundancies. We've had them all pencilled in since January. Dick Walker included.

Prin What redundancies?

Kite For the merger. With the Poly. All came together very smoothly this afternoon. Well, you knew it was on the cards, didn't you? University didn't have a leg to stand on.

Prin What on earth do you think you're talking about?

Kite Come on, Peggy. You know exactly what I'm talking about. You've known for months. You haven't made things any easier by your attitude, of course. I'd like to have had your creative input, but well, I respect your desire not to get involved.

Prin (*standing very still*) You've really done it. You've destroyed the college.

Kite There'll be a transition period, of course. It'll all be very smooth. We'll gradually absorb the Science Education side into the Poly structure, great advantages on both sides, Hedley Stafford's being very accommodating. The old house and the grounds were a key point, of course. Middle management training and conference centre. We're getting some Japanese and Hong Kong financial input there. It's all very exciting. Cynically it might be seen as asset-stripping, but I like to think of it as rationalization and enhancement. Bloody hell Peggy, we'll even have an eighteen-hole golf course here! No building on these grounds, I know that's something dear to your heart!

Prin There must be some misunderstanding. Those are the playing fields. This college specializes in physical education. The little men with their golf trolleys will get in the way of my athletes, surely someone could have had the wit to have foreseen that!

Kite Well, yes they did. Decision went on the other way, I'm afraid. Dr Boyle put up some very strong arguments for the PE Wing.

Prin Oh, I'm sure he did.

Kite But, well, as you know, DES thinking is that PE should be concentrated into two of three centres of excellence . . .

Prin And is this college not a centre of excellence?

Kite Yes of course it is. But it's been, how shall I put it, a bit out on a limb in recent years.

Prin We were always out on a limb.

Kite Well. Yes.

Prin We were always . . . exceptional.

Kite I need hardly say how sorry I am about this personally, Peggy.

Prin No, I don't think that will be necessary. Because you're not in fact sorry at all, you're enjoying every moment of this, aren't you?

Kite I've looked forward to it for a long time, if you want to know the truth.

Prin Good! Well done. Don't you feel better for that?

Kite Not particularly. Never really been happy about my relations with you, to be frank. Don't like feelings to get in the way. Never really help, do they? I mean I'm a doer, I like to get things done, I like to get on with my life. And, well, you and I go back a long way, Peggy, we've been through good times and bad, we've rubbed along reasonably well, but it's always been tricky. Feelings, you see. Can't help it. Always had a very strong feeling for you, Peggy.

Prin And what feeling was that?

Kite I bloody well hate you. Always have.

Prin Splendid. Thank you. D'you know, I think I'd like you out of here now.

Kite Yes, I can understand that. Er, just one more point.

Prin Yes?

Kite Afraid we weren't able to deliver on the Deputy Directorship. Of the Poly. You won't be too surprised or disappointed about that, I trust. Know you had your doubts about working with Hedley Stafford.

Prin I didn't have any doubts. I simply refused to have anything to do with the idea.

Kite Yes. Well, as it turned out, Hedley felt exactly the same. It's early retirement, I'm afraid. As from September first. We'll make the usual arrangement. They're quite generous, as you know.

Prin It's called the Crombie Scheme isn't it? Sounds like an undertaker's overcoat, don't you think? D'you think it'll keep me warm?

Kite Er . . . we've asked John Boyle to take over as Acting Principal for the transition period. He's been very helpful throughout the negotiations. Good man to deal with. He'll provide the continuity.

Prin Dr Bile. What a brilliant stroke. I congratulate you on it. It's strange. I didn't think you had the imagination. (*She turns and looks at him. Not "one of her looks". More open. Wondering*)

Kite (*disconcerted*) Well. Never easy, this sort of thing. (*He looks at his watch*) I've got another meeting. Um . . . if I . . . I just thought I should . . . No. Right.

He turns and goes

Prin stands very still, her hands by her sides. Her right arm is trembling slightly. It stops. Slowly she brings it up across her shoulder. Then the left arm, same movement

Prin (*musingly, as if trying it out for size*) "I am certain of nothing but the holiness of the heart's affections and the truth of the imagination." Yes. And all the rest, all the rest is bloody well immaterial. (*She strides to the drinks, pours herself a good one, and tosses it down. She grins*) Prin is herself again.

Dibs comes in

Oh there you are, Little Dibs, you've missed all the fun. They're all back in the stables now, mucking out. I do prefer the view in the late afternoon. The shadows are so enormous. Licking up the grass like great long tongues. I was quite transported. Then some fool came and interrupted me with some boring administrative reshuffle, my God the things people find to waste their time with. D'you know, I definitely think I'm coming round to Oninka Small. Julie Cinnamon *is* quite extraordinary, but I am beginning to think there's such a thing as too much symmetry. What's your opinion?

Dibs I heard the news. I'm really very sorry, Prin.

Pause

D'you want a cuddle?

Prin No, little Dibs, I don't think I do want a cuddle just now.

Pause

I really didn't think they'd do it, you know.

Dibs (*gently*) You must have seen it coming.

Prin (*impatiently*) Yes of course I saw it coming, I simply dismissed it from my mind, that's all. It's immaterial. It's inconvenient, but it's immaterial. You were quite right, Dibs. They are all figments of the imagination, all those people, God knows now what possessed me to invent them, but I can invent others. Let them all go, let them creep off and shrivel away, Walker, Kite, his bicycle, Bile. Especially Bile.

Dibs Prin.

Prin Did you know he's going to be Acting Principal?

Dibs Yes, I did in point of fact.

Prin What a grotesque conceit, eh, Dibs? I'm really grateful to Kite for that one. How d'you think he'll redecorate this room?

Dibs (*reluctantly*) No idea.

Prin Skins on the wall, of course, neatly graded by size, stoats on the left, shrews on the right, all pinned out by their little hands and feet. And let's see, a new desk. What would his taste be, Dibs? You seem to see much more of him than I do these days.

Dibs Oh, I don't know. Don't think he's fussy really.

Prin Dr Bile is *very* fussy. Dr Bile leaves nothing to chance. Stainless steel, I think, for the desk. So practical. So easy to swab down with surgical spirit. Do Bile for me, Dibs. Do Bile at his stainless steel desk, receiving visitors. Interrupted at his nameless rites.

Dibs (*shaking her head*) No. I wish you'd stop this.

Prin You're getting very dull, little Dibs. Don't you think I deserve a little cheering up?

Dibs That wouldn't do any good. Besides . . . I don't think I can do that any more.

Prin Ah. It didn't *have* to be you, Dibs. It *was* you . . . it turned *out* to be you . . . but that day, when I made everybody stop, when I made everybody watch you move . . . that day when I chose you . . . there really wasn't anything all that special about you.

Dibs Good.

Prin I don't say it could have been any of them, that would be a bit too strong, but it could have been any of quite a little number. Watch . . . er . . . er . . . *Dorothy* move, I said. (*As if in doubt whom to choose*) And so they did.

Long pause

Dibs What are you going to do now?

Prin I carry my world with me. I could do anything. We might stay in Greece. Get a large villa. Write in the mornings. Sit under the fig trees in the afternoons. Invite a few fools round in the evening. Laugh about them when they've gone home at night. Receive the odd pilgrim.

Dibs Prin: I said I wasn't going to come to Greece this year.

Prin Yes, yes, I know, but I overlooked it. Everyone's entitled to a fit of pique. Come on, little pigwig. I understand these things.

Dibs Well, um, I meant it in point of fact. Not a whim.

Prin Oh.

Dibs You see for one thing I'm still Vice-Principal. There's an awful lot to be sorted out in the vac, what with all the changes. John's very good on the politics and admin and all, but he hasn't a clue about the pastoral side.

Prin You're going to stay here in the vac. You're going to stay here in the vac, working with the vile doctor. Oh, no, Dibs. That's too much. I won't let them do that to you.

Dibs I don't mind doing it, actually. Anyway, I've said I will now. They were all very grateful. They said they didn't know what they would have done if I'd refused. They said I was indispensable. They said they counted on me.

Prin (*something in the voice*) I count on you.

Dibs (*quite affectionate*) No you don't. Not really. I'm just a figment of your imagination, you said so yourself. Could have been anybody. Watch ... er ... er ... Dorothy move.

Prin But it *was* you, and the extraordinary thing is, now I cannot imagine myself having chosen anyone else. I care about you, Dibs. I can't abandon you to that clammy little man.

Dibs Actually ... as I've been trying to tell you all day ... he's not so bad. I didn't care for him much at first, and there's some things about him still that sniff really is awful, but he's trying to work on it ...

Prin Oh, good, what's he doing, increasing the volume? Widening the total range?

Dibs What I was going to say was, when you work with someone every day you do get to know them a lot better.

Prin Oh really? I must write that down, Dibs.

Dibs And the things that irritate you at first don't actually seem to matter so much after a while.

Prin Oh, you find that, do you? I actually really find the reverse, that some little irritating things seem increasingly how shall I put it iffy and naff in point of fact.

Dibs And well, I found I was actually enjoying some of our conversations. He does have a few things to talk about besides his rats and his newts, believe it or not, and more to the point he seemed quite interested in what I had to say.

Prin Well, of course he *was*. The little shit was plotting against me.

Dibs We didn't talk about you. I know you find that hard to credit, but it's true. Well, anyway. About six months ago, I was feeling pretty low down. You'd been particularly bloody about something or other, and I was drooping about the place, and he actually noticed and asked me out for a meal to cheer me up. So I thought that was nice of him, why not, so I went. Yes, all right, grilled squirrel's pancreas, heard it . . . we had a nice ordinary meal and he turned out to be very kind in a way and rather shy.

Prin Shy. Bile shy. That's a new one.

Dibs So we did it again. As often as we could, in fact, I got to look forward to it. Mostly when you were in Oxford with your old cronies; you know the evenings you wouldn't take me to because I wouldn't be up to the rapier wit and the subtle allusions.

Prin I didn't want you to be bored, that's all.

Dibs Oh, fine. This is little Dibs, she'll make you an omelette. And, well, meals, talks, coffee, going on quite late sometimes, and eventually rather to both our surprise I think, he asked me how I'd feel about going to bed with him. And I thought, well, I'll give it a try. I don't suppose I'll ever get another chance.

Prin And it was, of course, an earth-shaking revelation that changed the course of your whole life.

Dibs No, it was pretty hopeless actually. John hadn't had much experience of women, and he was very shy and anxious, and of course I'd had no experience at all of men . . . and actually I don't think men do understand very much about pleasing women anyway. But it wasn't, in the end, too embarrassing and dreadful. We even managed to have a bit of a giggle about it. And he didn't get too discouraged, he wanted to try again, and I found I did too. We bought a book.

Prin You bought a *book*?

Dibs Yes, it was called *The Joy of Sex*. It was a bit, you know, ambitious and polemical, and the illustrations were a bit off-putting because they didn't look a bit like us, but by and large it was quite a useful purchase. I think it saved us quite a bit of time. I feel a bit rotten about not telling you all this before, but at first I didn't know whether it was going to *be* anything, and lately, well . . . it's been as if you were stopping me. And then this morning when you made me do him, the rat and that, I was sure you must know, and that's why you were doing it.

Prin I didn't know.

Dibs That's amazing. I mean we've been as discreet as we could, but I should think everyone has noticed.

Prin Do you? I must say that lends the memory of recent weeks a certain piquancy. I must have been the source of some amusement.

Dibs No. I really don't think you were. You mean you didn't notice anything?

Prin We see what we choose to see, don't we?

Dibs All that trouble with the gloomy kippers? All that sudden running off to puke? Didn't it occur to you I might be pregnant? Well, I am, Prin.

Prin Dr Bile has got you pregnant? (*After a pause*) What a fecund place this college has become. And how do you feel, about being pregnant by Dr Bile?

Dibs Boyle, Prin. I feel all right about it. I sort of love him in a way.

Prin You sort of love him in a way.

Dibs That's right. We're going to be married in a point of fact.

Pause

Prin Dibs. Dorothy. Don't leave me.

Pause

Dibs Sorry. Can't be helped. I've just sort of, you know, had enough, now of all your stuff. I've had enough of being invented. He isn't frightfully clever and he'll never make me laugh the way you do, and I don't think I'm going to spend much time being amazed and delighted, and in fact I'm absolutely scared shitless that I'll be bored to tears.

Prin (*not looking at her*) I love you.

Dibs Or something, what it is, finally . . . I'm not a prima donna. I'm a job lot.

Prin stands looking at the audience. Dibs waits to see if she is going to say anything. She doesn't

Dibs turns and goes out quietly

Prin comes forward. Looks out into the audience, as if for one of her lectures. But she looks a bit uncertain. She clears her throat

Prin I think we might as well dispense with the formalities. In this lecture I propose to deal with the holiness of the heart's affections and the truth of the imagination, especially as they effect the body swayed to music; not to mention the brightening glance. Not to mention that. (*She peers into the audience and frowns slightly*) You have doubtless come to listen to me this evening because you're interested in these matters, you're fellow workers in this rewarding field, because you've read my books, because you're initiates in the advanced study of human movement, and consequently involved in the pursuit of excellence. Well, let's assume that you are. I have a great many speaking engagements, no doubt someone told me the name of the body I'm addressing, but I have no recollection of it, no recollection at all, not to put too fine a point on it, you look a pretty rum bunch to me. I'm not by any chance in the *Poly*, am I? You'll have to forgive me. I've had a rather tiresome day. As soon as I've finished with you lot I'll have a cigarette and a really big stiffener and feel much better. However. "I am certain of nothing but the holiness of the heart's affections and the truth of the imagination." "I am certain of nothing but the holiness . . ." (*She stops, as if for the first time considering the significance of this bit*) I am certain of. I am certain. I am. I. (*She pauses*) Listen. One day, one day years ago I came into a room full of dancers. Go into yourselves, I said to the dancers. Find your point of stillness. And move when you have to move. And then they moved. And I watched them. And then I said: everybody stop. Watch Dorothy move. Watch Dorothy move. Watch . . . *Dorothy* move.

CURTAIN

FURNITURE AND PROPERTY LIST

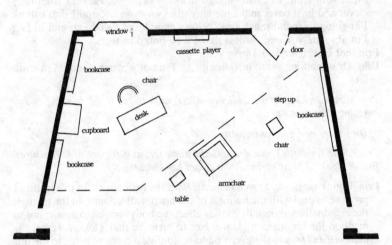

ACT I

On stage: Desk. *On it:* intercom, papers, pens
Chairs
Small table. *On it:* ashtray, cigarettes, lighter
Cupboard. *In it:* bottle of whisky, soda syphon, glasses
Cassette player with tape in, other tapes
Gown

Off stage: Long table covered with dark cloth, bowl of flowers on top **(Stage Management)**
2 chairs **(Stage Management)**
File of papers **(Dibs)**

Personal: **Prin:** wrist-watch ⎱ required throughout
Kite: wrist-watch ⎰

ACT II

Strike: Dirty glass

Set: Long table with cloth, flowers, papers, pens
3 chairs
Briefcase with papers for **Boyle**

LIGHTING PLOT

Property fittings required: nil

Interior. An office. The same scene throughout

ACT I   Morning

To open: General interior lighting

Cue 1   **Prin** turns her back and walks upstage   (Page 24)
          Fade lights

ACT II   Afternoon

To open: General interior lighting

No cues

EFFECTS PLOT

ACT I

Cue 1	**Prin:** "Some things, thank God, don't change." *Intercom bleeps*	(Page 2)
Cue 2	**Dibs:** "Well ..." *Intercom bleeps*	(Page 3)
Cue 3	**Boyle** turns and goes *Dog barks and growls off*	(Page 12)
Cue 4	**Prin** (*on phone*): "I'll see Mr Walker now." *Growling and snarling off*	(Page 14)
Cue 5	**Kite** goes out *Flurry of growling, off*	(Page 22)

ACT II

Cue 6	**Dibs** switches tape on *Pause, then music—Chopin*	(Page 34)
Cue 7	**Dibs** switches tape off *Cut music*	(Page 34)
Cue 8	**Prin:** "Tears before bedtime." *Barking and growling, off*	(Page 35)

MADE AND PRINTED IN GREAT BRITAIN BY
LATIMER TREND & COMPANY LTD PLYMOUTH

MADE IN ENGLAND